CW00428547

THE COTSWOLDS
BROADWAY and CHIPPING CAMPDEN

JOHN CURTIS
Text by Richard Ashby

SALMON

INTRODUCTION

Broadway and Chipping Campden lie either side of the boundary between Worcestershire and Gloucestershire. They share the same honey coloured limestone and domestic architecture but their origins and history are different. Broadway grew up at the bottom of the escarpment where the traffic on the Worcester to London road stopped for refreshment and additional horses before ascending Fish Hill, whereas Chipping Campden developed as a market town and was particularly important in medieval times as a trading centre for wool.

The wool industry declined and patterns of trade changed. The railway by-passed Chipping Campden and ignored Broadway. But it was this very decline and the absence of development which made possible a remarkable renaissance.

Towards the end of the 19th century William Morris, the artist, designer and English socialist, was preaching a new gospel of beauty and harmony, honest craftsmanship and simple living. While staying at Broadway Tower he walked out one evening with his friends and found his ideal and inspiration in the little town at the bottom of the hill. It was not long before artists and craftsmen came to live and work here. Broadway gained a reputation as one of the most beautiful places in England while Chipping Campden became a centre for fine craftsmanship. Both have an important place in the history of the Arts and Crafts movement and remain an inspiration to a new generation of lovers of the picturesque and beautiful.

Broadway from Fish Hill

Memorial Cross, Broadway

Broadway is situated where the Worcester to London road ascends the escarpment of the Cotswolds out of the Vale of Evesham. In coaching days this was the point at which additional horses were harnessed to tackle the steep incline. This simple cross on the green commemorates the fifty-nine men from the village killed in the two World Wars.

Telephone Boxes, Broadway

The red telephone box is something of a design classic. This version was designed in 1936 by Sir Giles Gilbert Scott, the eminent architect. Many thousands were erected and it became a familiar part of Britain's street scene. Many have now gone but somehow it seems right that they should remain here. Like Broadway itself they have become a part of England's heritage.

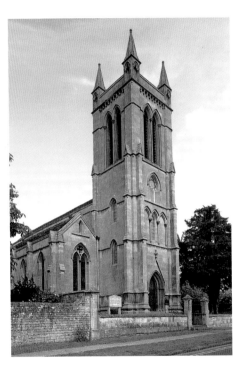

Church of St Michael, Broadway
Broadway's original parish church,
St Eadburgha's, is a little way out of the
village and St Michael's was built in 1839
to replace a 'chapel of ease', which previously
stood here. It is an early example of a church
built under the influence of the 'Tractarians',
who sought to bring the Church of England
back to its Catholic roots.

High Street, Broadway
The prosperity of Broadway has always
depended on visitors. There were once some
thirty-three inns here, many serving the
coaching trade, and the shops served both
the traveller and the local people. Today
the visitor is tempted by the galleries,
antique shops and tea rooms which
line the broad High Street.

Wisteria Cottage, Broadway
Of all the cottages which line Broadway's main street, perhaps the most photographed is Wisteria Cottage, with its gnarled branches and profusion of purple blooms in late spring entwining the mullioned windows and mingling with the honey-coloured stone.

High Street, Broadway
The Anglo Saxon name, *Bradanwege*, derives from an estate owned by Brada, rather than to the width of the long High Street. However it is one of the widest in England and is lined with a wonderful array of old houses dating from the 16th and 17th centuries.

Mile Stone, High Street, Broadway

With the development of the stage coach, Broadway became a major coaching centre. Here fresh horses had to be put on to the coaches for the pull up Fish Hill while the passengers refreshed themselves at the inns. At one time there were seven daily stage coaches passing through; the Worcester to London journey taking seventeen hours.

16th Century Cottages, Broadway

Broadway has been an inspiration for many artists, musicians and writers. It became something of a haven for American artists. Francis Millet said it was a 'quaint reflection of a long ago country village' and John Singer Sargent painted his famous picture *Carnation, Lily, Lily Rose* here.

The Lygon Arms, Broadway

It is almost certain that this was originally a large manor house, but by the 16th century it had become The White Hart Inn. Its name was changed to The Lygon Arms in 1826 when the new owner, General Lygon, who had fought at Waterloo, installed his steward to be the landlord. Charles I is reputed to have stayed here.

Old Corner, Broadway

The art of cutting conifer bushes into fantastic designs goes back to Roman times. It has been in and out of fashion over the centuries. Much loved in the 17th century, a great deal was swept away in the 18th. In the 19th century topiary became associated with the cottage garden style under the influence of the Arts and Crafts Movement.

Old Cottages, Broadway
There is something very appealing about the vernacular architecture of the Cotswolds. The combination of the honey-coloured stone with thatch or stone tiled roofs, the whole covered in a profusion of flowers, for many, epitomises the ideal rural retreat.

Broadway Tower
The hill above the town has always been known as 'Beacon Hill', a place where a beacon was lit in times of danger or rejoicing. The tower was built in 1797 by the Earl of Coventry. It has been described as a 'folly', a building which has no discernable practical use, but one story has it that a fire would be lit here to signal that Lord Coventry's coach was on its way to his home, at nearby Croome Court. It was sold to the printer Sir Thomas Phillips in 1827. Later in the century William Morris came to stay here and with two friends walked down the hill to explore the village below for the first time.

Church of St Eadburgha, Bury End

Built around 1200 AD, this was Broadway's first parish church and served the village until the early part of the 19th century. It is situated about three-quarters of a mile from the centre of the village, possibly because this was where the ancient trackway from London to Wales, the forerunner of the modern road, began its ascent of the Cotswolds. With the population increasing it was decided to build the new church, St Michael's, in the village itself. The old church might have suffered the fate of many others in similar situations and there were moves to demolish it on the completion of the new. Happily, this did not happen, the church survived and occasional services are still held here. The dedication of the church is usual. St Eadburgha was a grand-daughter of King Alfred, and the Abbess of St Peter's, Winchester.

Snowshill Manor Garden

Snowshill Manor dates from around 1500. It is built from honey-coloured stone and has lovely gables and chimneys. It had been extensively altered in the 17th and 18th centuries but by the end of the 19th was largely derelict. Charles Paget Wade, was an enthusiast for the values of the Arts and Crafts Movement, restored the manor in 1919 using traditional methods and local craftsmen wherever he could. At the same time the fine gardens were laid out and designed 'as a series of separate courts, sunny ones contrasting with shady ones and different moods'. It is the first garden to be managed by the National Trust on organic principles.

Snowshill

Snowshill is situated in a fold of the hills, on the Cotswold Edge where the scarp falls away in to the Vale of Evesham. Almost all the village is old and built of local stone. Charles Paget Wade, restorer of Snowshill Manor, is buried in the grounds of the church. Above the village, some fifty-three acres have been planted with lavender.

Stanton

Less than a hundred years ago, this perfectly preserved Cotswold village, was in serious decline and at risk of dereliction but, fortunately, in 1906 the estate was bought by Sir Philip Stott, an architect, and he began a sympathetic restoration. Some of the gabled houses of honey-coloured stone, with their lovely cottage gardens, have date stones built into them showing when they were constructed, and sometimes, the initials of their builder. Many date from the 16th and 17th centuries, regarded by some as the best period of Cotswold vernacular architecture. At the centre of the village is the market cross, the 18th century shaft standing on a medieval base.

Stanway House

The gardens of Stanway House were originally laid out in the early 18th century by the pioneer of landscape gardening, Charles Bridgeman. At their centre is a great canal fed by a cascade, the largest in Britain. The new fountain, opened in 2004, rises to 300 ft. It is the tallest gravity-driven fountain in the world. The ornate 17th century gateway guards the entrance to the house which was often visited by J M Barrie, the author of *Peter Pan*, who would captain the local cricket team. Buried in the church is Thomas Dover, captain of the privateer, 'The Duke', and remembered as the man who rescued Alexander Selkirk, the inspiration for Daniel Defoe's *Robinson Crusoe*.

Chipping Campden

This beautifully preserved town had also fallen into great decay by the end of the 19th century and its population had halved. The architect and visionary C R Ashbee found here the perfect place for the workmen and their families of his School of Arts and Crafts and moved them from London's East End in 1902, thus establishing a tradition of fine craftsmanship, which continues to this day. Later, other architects helped form the Campden Trust, which has done much work in restoring the town to its former beauty.

Almshouses, Chipping Campden

There is a unity about Cotswold towns and villages which results in buildings separated by several centuries having an affinity of style and materials. These 17th century almshouses mingle quite happily with the 14th to 18th century buildings around them. They were a gift of Sir Baptist Hicks, the first Lord Campden.

Church of St James, Chipping Campden

The great parish church was entirely remodelled in the 14th and 15th centuries in the latest Perpendicular style to reflect the prosperity and civic pride of the town, which had grown rich on the wool trade. In the floor of the chancel are four memorial brasses, including one to William Greville, 'the flower of the wool merchants of all England'.

The Gatehouse, Campden House Chipping Campden

Sir Baptist Hicks, a great merchant, amassed sufficient wealth to enable him to lend money to both James I and Charles I. He was a great benefactor to the town and built himself a fine mansion, Campden House, near the church. Unfortunately, during the English Civil War the army of Prince Rupert, the Royalist Commander-in-chief, set fire to it to prevent it from falling into the hands of Cromwell's army. Today, only the gateway and lodges, two garden pavilions (now holiday homes) and shattered fragments of the house itself, hint at the grandeur that was Campden House.

High Street and Market Hall
Chipping Campden

The town of Campden received its charter in 1185, which entitled it to hold a weekly market. Within a century it was famous, drawing traders from a wide area, and the town's name had acquired the addition of the Anglo Saxon word for 'market'. It has since been known as Chipping Campden. By the 14th century it was famous for its wool, the foundation of the town's prosperity. The High Street has been described as the most perfect in England. The Market Hall, another gift of Sir Baptist Hicks, was built in 1627 to shelter those who were selling cheese, eggs and butter. Sir Baptist's coat of arms is displayed on one end.

Dover's Hill, Chipping Campden

Robert Dover established his 'Olimpick Games' in 1612, with the permission of King James I, in a natural amphitheatre on this hill above Chipping Campden. They became very famous and both William Shakespeare and Ben Jonson mention them. Suppressed by the Puritans and then the local vicar, they were revived in 1951 and have been held every Spring since.

Hidcote Manor Gardens

The American Lawrence Johnston came to Hidcote in 1907 with his wealthy mother, who bought the property for her son on account of his poor health. The son soon became a keen gardener and the garden he created here is one of England's greatest, following in the tradition of Gertrude Jekyll.

Kiftsgate Court Gardens

Within a few miles of each other there are three fine gardens, all created in the early 20th century and all showing the influence of the Arts and Crafts Movement on English gardening. Kiftsgate's wonderful gardens are the product of three generations of women gardeners. It was begun by Mrs Heather Muir in the 1920's, with help from near neighbour Lawrence Johnston of Hidcote, was continued by her daughter and is now looked after by her grand-daughter. Before 1920 there was little besides a paved formal garden by the house, but over the years a whole series of gardens were created, like Hidcote and Snowshill, each with its own theme and character.

Willersey

Over the border in Gloucestershire but
within a mile or so of Broadway is Willersey,
another lovely picture-postcard Cotswold
village. Its houses are built either side of
a long village green in the centre of which
is the village pond overlooked by Pool House
with its stately stone pillars.

Published and Printed in Great Britain by
J. Salmon Ltd., Sevenoaks, Kent TN13 1BB. © 2007
Website: www.jsalmon.com. Telephone: 01732 452381.
Email: enquiries@jsalmon.co.uk.

Design by John Curtis. Text and photographs © John Curtis.

ISBN 1-84640-101-1
Title page photograph: Doorway at Stanton.
Front cover photograph: 16th Century Cottages at Broadway.
Back cover photograph: Cottage at Chipping Campden.